Letters from a Father to his Daughter

Jawaharlal Nehru

DIAMOND BOOKS
www.diamondbooks.in

Publisher : **Diamond Pocket Books (P) Ltd.**
X-30, Okhla Industrial Area,
Phase-II, New Delhi-110020
Phone : 011-40712200
E-mail : wecare@diamondbooks.in
Website : www.diamondbooks.in
Edition : 2025
Printed by : Repro (India)

Letters from a Father to his Daughter
Author - *Jawaharlal Nehru*

To Indira
to whom these letters are written

Introduction

Letters from a Father to His Daughter is a charming collection of letters written by Jawaharlal Nehru to his young daughter, Indira Priyadarshini (later Indira Gandhi), during his imprisonment in 1928. Jawaharlal Nehru's correspondence with his daughter, Indira Gandhi, is often regarded as a beautiful reflection of his thoughts on education, progress, and humanism, which resonate with individuals from various walks of life. These letters, though intended for a child, offer profound insights into Nehru's vision of India, history, and the world around him. His knowledge and understanding about all these subjects was commendable. He wanted to convey and share all this to his daughter through these letters. Moreover he loved nature much so he focussed on the information related to nature.

The book is a beautiful blend of personal affection and intellectual depth. Nehru, separated from his daughter by distance and circumstances, communicates his thoughts through letters filled with fascinating descriptions of nature, science, history, and human progress. He talks to her not as a father, but as a guide, teaching her about the world, its wonders, and the importance of curiosity. The letters reflect Nehru's love for learning and his belief in the power of education, particularly for young minds. He introduces Indira to the natural world, explains the principles of science, and delves into the realms of art, culture, and history, all while weaving a sense of hope for India's future.

Nehru wanted to bridge the emotional and intellectual gap created by his imprisonment, all while imparting his ideas to his daughter, who was far from him. The book's tone, though informal, conveys Nehru's serious concerns about India's future, the importance of self-reliance, and the necessity of a scientific and rational approach to problems.

In essence, *Letters from a Father to His Daughter* is more than just a father's correspondence with his daughter; it is a valuable literary work that reflects Nehru's commitment to education, humanism, and a progressive India.

-Publisher

N. K. Verma
nk@dpb.in

Contents

Preface to Third Edition

Most children idolize their parents, but not all parents are as good companions as mine were. My father was interested in everything and delighted in sharing his enthusiasm. I was full of questions and this enabled him to tell me about the world, and the men and women who inhabited it and who have moved others by their ideas and actions, and through literature and art. Above all he loved to speak and write about our wonderful country, its early achievements and grandeur, and the later decline and bondage. One thought was uppermost in his mind and that was freedom—freedom not only for India but for all peoples of the world.

The letters in this book, written when I was eight or nine, deal with the beginnings of the earth and of man's awareness of himself. They were not merely letters to be read and put away. They brought a fresh outlook and aroused a feeling of concern for people and interest in the world around. They taught one to treat nature as a book. I spent absorbing hours studying stones and plants, the lives of insects and at night, the stars.

The letters have earlier appeared in book form in different languages, but I am sure this attractive reprint will appeal to children and will open new vistas for them as the original letters did for me.

New Delhi
1 November 1973

Indira Gandhi

Preface to Second Edition

I had hesitated long before I decided to place these letters before a wider audience than they were originally intended for. But the reception which a kindly press and a kindlier public gave to them emboldened me and quieted my doubts and fears. The first edition has long been exhausted and even the author of the *Letters* has no copy left. A second edition is therefore being brought out. A few minor errors have been corrected; otherwise there is no change.

Emboldened by the welcome given to this little book, I had thought of adding to these letters. But I had allied myself to a jealous mistress and her service left me little time or inclination to dabble in other matters. Last year when I went to Naini prison, the thought came. back to me and time was not lacking. But prison letters are not frequent and a prison does not provide books of reference. And above all, my mind was too full of the making of history, as it was being made from day to day in India, for me to think of the dead past. I came out of jail and returned to it after a brief week of absence; and again the months passed. On the first of January of this year, however, I made a New Year resolve to continue these letters. I made some progress, but too soon, on January 26, I was suddenly discharged. Domestic affliction and the whirlpool of public affairs caught me in swirl and cast me hither and thither. And I await again the peace and quiet of the prison to continue this task.

Meanwhile, Indira grows and I might not keep pace for long with her growing knowledge.

Allahabad
October 1931

Jawaharlal Nehru

Foreword to First Edition

These letters were written to my daughter Indira in the summer of 1928 when she was in the Himalayas at Mussoorie and I was in the plains below. They were personal letters addressed to a little girl, ten years of age. But friends, whose advice I value, have seen some virtue in them, and have suggested that I might place them before a wider audience. I do not know if other boys and girls will appreciate them. But I hope that such of them as read these letters may gradually begin to think of this world of ours as a large family of nations. And I hope also, though with diffidence, that they may find in the reading of them a fraction of the pleasure that I had in the writing of them.

The letters end abruptly. The long summer had come to an end and Indira had to come down from the mountains. And there was no Mussoorie or other hill station for her in the summer of 1929. The last three letters begin a new period and are somewhat out of place by themselves. But I have included them as there is little chance of my adding to them.

I realize that the letters being in English, their circle of appeal is limited. The fault is entirely mine. I can only remedy it now by having a translation made.

Allahabad
November 1929

Jawaharlal Nehru

The Book of Nature

When you and I are together, you often ask me questions about many things and I try to answer them. Now that you are at Mussoorie and I am in Allahabad we cannot have these talks. I am therefore going to write to you from time to time short accounts of the story of our earth and the many countries, great and small, into which it is divided. You have read a little about English history and Indian history. But England is only a little island and India, though a big country, is only a small part of the earth's surface. If we want to know something about the story of this world of ours we must think of all the countries and all the peoples that have inhabited it, and not merely of one little country where we may have been born.

I am afraid I can only tell you very little in these letters of mine. But that little, I hope, will interest you and make you think of the world as a whole, and of other peoples in it as our brothers and sisters. When you grow up you will read about the story of the earth and her peoples in fat books and you will find it more interesting than any other story or novel that you may have read.

You know, of course, that our earth is very, very old—millions and millions of years old. And for a long, long time there were no men or women living in it. Before the men came there were only animals, and before the animals there was a time when no kind of life existed on the earth. It is difficult to imagine this world of ours, which is so full today of all kinds of animals and men, to be without them. But scientists and those who have studied and thought a great deal about these matters tell us that there was a time when the earth was too hot for any living being to live on it. And if we read their books and study the rocks and the fossils (the remains of old animals), we can ourselves see that this must have been so.

You read history in books. But in old times when men did not exist, surely no books could have been written. How then can we find out what happened then? We cannot merely sit down and imagine everything. This would be very interesting for we could imagine anything we wanted to and would thus make up the most beautiful fairy tales. But this need not be true as it would not be based on any facts that we had seen. But although we have no books written in those far-off days, fortunately we have some things which tell us a great deal as well, almost as a book would. We have rocks and mountains and seas and stars and rivers and deserts and fossils of old animals. These and other like things are our books for the earth's early story. And the real way to understand this story is not merely to read about it in other people's books but to go to the great Book of Nature itself. You will, I hope, soon begin to learn how to read this story from the rocks and mountains. Imagine how fascinating it is! Every little stone that you see lying on the road or on the mountainside may be a little page in nature's book and may be able to tell you something if you only knew how to read it. To be able to read any language, Hindi or Urdu or English, you have to learn its alphabet. So also you must learn the alphabet of nature before you can read her story in her books of stone and rock. Even now perhaps you know a little how to read this.

If you see a little round shiny pebble, does it not tell you something? How did it get round and smooth and shiny, without any corners or rough edges? If you break a big rock into small bits, each bit is rough and has corners and rough edges. It is not at all like a round smooth pebble. How then did the pebble become so round and smooth and shiny? It will be tell you its story if you have good eyes to see and ears to hear it. It tells you that once upon a time, it may be long ago, it was a bit of a rock, just like the bit you may break from a big rock or stone with plenty of edges and corners. Probably it rested on some mountainside. Then came the rain and washed it down to the little valley where it found a mountain stream, which pushed it on and on till it reached a little river. And the little river took it to the big river. And all the while, it rolled at the bottom of the river and its edges were worn away and its rough surface made smooth and shiny. So it became the pebble that you see. Somehow, the river left it behind and you found it. If the river had carried it on, it would have become smaller and smaller till at last it became a grain of sand and joined its brothers at the seaside to make a beautiful beach where little children can play and make castles out of the sand.

If a little pebble can tell you so much, how much more could we learn from all the rocks and mountains and the many other things we see around us?

❐

How Early History was Written

In my letter to you yesterday, I pointed out that we have to study the early story of the earth from the book of nature. The book consists of everything that you see around you—the rocks and mountains and valleys and rivers and seas and volcanoes. This book is always open before us but few of us pay any attention to it or try to read it! If we learnt how to read it and understand it, how many interesting stories it could tell us! The stories we would read about in its pages of stone would be more interesting than a fairy tale.

And so from this book of nature we would learn something of those far-off days when no man or animal lived on this earth of ours. As we read on, we shall see the first animals appear, and later more animals. And then will come man and woman, but they will be very different from the men and women we see today. They will be savages, not very different from animals. Gradually they will gather experience and begin to think. The power of thought will make them really different from the animals. It will be a real power which will make them stronger than the biggest and fiercest animal. You see today a little man sit on top of a great big elephant and make him do what he wills. The elephant is big and strong, far stronger than the little *mahaut* sitting on his neck. But the *mahaut* can think, and because he can think he becomes the master and the elephant is his servant. So, as thought grew in man he became cleverer and wiser. He found out many things—how to make a fire, how to cultivate the land and grow his food, how to make cloth to wear and houses to live in. Many men and women used to live together and so we had the first cities. Before the cities were made, men used to wander about from place to place, probably living in some kind of tents. They did not know then how to grow their food from the land. They had no rice therefore, nor did they have any wheat, from which bread is made. There were no vegetables and most of the things you eat today were not known then. Perhaps there were some wild nuts and fruits which men ate but mostly they must have lived on animals which they killed.

As cities grew people learnt many beautiful arts. They also learnt how to write. But for a long time there was no paper to write on and people used to write on the bark of the *Bhojpatra* tree—I think this is called the birch in English—or they wrote on palm leaves. Even now you will find in some libraries whole books written in. those far-off days on the leaves of the palm tree. Then came paper and it was easier to write. But there were no printing presses and books could not be printed off in their thousands as is done today. A book could only be written once and then copied out by hand laboriously. Of course, there could not be many books. You could not just go to a bookseller or a bookstall to buy a book. You had to get someone to copy it and this took a long time. But people in those days wrote beautifully and we have today many books in our libraries which were beautifully written by hand. In India especially we have books in Sanskrit and Persian and Urdu. Often the man who copied the book made flowers and drawings on the sides of the page.

With the growth of cities, gradually countries and nations were formed. People who lived near each other in one country naturally got to know each other better. They thought they were better than others who lived in other countries and, very foolishly, they fought with these others. They did not realize, and people do not realize even now, that fighting and killing each other are about the most stupid things that people can do. It does good to nobody.

To learn the story of these early days of cities and countries we sometimes get old books. But there are not many of these. Other things help us. The kings and emperors of old times used to have accounts of their reigns written on stone tablets and pillars. Books cannot last long. Their paper rots away and gets moth-eaten. But stones last much longer. Perhaps you remember seeing the great stone pillar of Ashoka in the Allahabad Fort. On this is cut out in stone a proclamation of Ashoka, who was a great king of India many hundreds of years ago. If you go to the museum in Lucknow you will find many stone tablets with words engraved on them.

In studying the old history of various countries, we shall learn of the great things that were done in China and Egypt long ago when the countries of Europe were full of savage tribes. We shall learn also of the great days of India when the Ramayana and Mahabharata were written and India was a rich and powerful country. Today, our country is very poor and a foreign people govern us. We are not free even in our own country and cannot do what we want. But this was not so always and perhaps if we try hard we may make our country free again, so that we may improve the lot of the poor, and make India as pleasant to live in as are some of the countries of Europe today.

In my next letter I shall begin this fascinating story of the earth from the very beginning.

❒

The Making of the Earth

You know that the earth goes round the sun and the moon goes round the earth. You know also perhaps that there are several other bodies which, like the earth, go round the sun. All these, including our earth, are called planets of the sun. The moon is called a satellite of the earth because it hangs on to it. The other planets have also got their satellites. The sun and the planets with their satellites form a happy family. This is called the solar system. Solar means belonging to the sun, and the sun being the father of all the planets the whole group is called the solar system.

At night, you see thousands of stars in the sky. Only a few of these are the planets and these are really not called stars at all. Can you distinguish between a planet and a star? The planets are really quite tiny, like our earth, compared to the stars but they look bigger in the sky because they are much nearer to us. Just as the moon, which is really quite a baby, looks so big because it is quite near to us. But the real way to distinguish the stars from the planets is to see if they twinkle or not. Stars twinkle, planets do not. That is because the planets only shine because they get the light of our sun. It is only the sunshine on the planets or the moon that we see. The real stars are like our sun. They shine of themselves because they are very hot and burning. In reality, our sun itself is a star, only it looks bigger as it is nearer and we see it as a great ball of fire.

So then our earth belongs to the family of the sun—the solar system. We think the earth is very big, and it is big compared to our tiny selves. It takes weeks and months to go from one part of it to another even in a fast train or steamer. But although it seems so big to us it is just like a speck of dust hanging in the air. The sun is millions of miles away and the other stars are even further away.

Astronomers, those people who study the stars, tell us that long, long ago the earth and all the planets were part of the sun. The sun was then, as it is now, a mass of flaming matter, terribly hot. Somehow little bits of the sun got loose and they shot out into the air. But they could not wholly get rid of their father, the sun. It was as if a rope was tied to them and they kept whirling round the sun. This strange force, which I have compared to a rope, is something which attracts little things to great. It is the force which makes things fall by their weight. The earth being the biggest thing near us attracts everything we have.

In this way our earth also shot out from the sun. It must have been very hot, with terribly hot gases and air all round it, but as it was very much smaller than the sun it started to cool. The sun also is getting less hot but it will take millions of years to cool down. The earth took much less time to cool. When it was hot, of course, nothing could live on it—no man or animal or plant or tree. Everything would have been burnt up then.

Just as a bit of the sun shot out and became the earth, so also a bit of the earth shot out and became the moon. Many people think that the moon came out of the great hollow which is now the Pacific Ocean, between America and Japan. So the earth started to cool. It took a long time over it. Gradually, the surface of the earth became cooler although the interior remained very hot. Even now if you go down a coal mine, it becomes hotter and hotter as you go down. Probably if you could go down deep enough inside the earth you would find it red hot. The moon also started to cool, and because it was much smaller than even the earth it cooled more quickly than the earth. It looks delightfully cool, does it not? It is called the 'cold moon'. Perhaps it is full of glaciers and ice fields.

When the earth cooled, all the water vapour in the air condensed into water and probably came down as rain. It must have rained a tremendous lot then. All this water filled the great hollows in the earth, and so the great oceans and seas were formed.

As the earth became cooler and the oceans also became cooler, it became possible for living things to exist on the earth's surface or in the sea. We shall discuss the early beginnings of life in the next letter.

❐

The First Living Things

We saw in our last letter that for a long time the earth must have been too hot for any living things to exist on it. When did life begin on the earth and what were the first living things? That is a very interesting question but it is also a very difficult question to answer. Let us first consider what life is. You will probably say that men are living beings and so are all animals. What about trees and shrubs and flowers and vegetables? Surely they are living also. They grow and drink up the water and breathe the air and die. The chief difference between a tree and an animal is that the tree does not move about. If you remember, I showed you some plants in Kew Gardens in London. These plants—orchids and pitcher plants—actually eat flies. Then there are some animals, like sponges, which live at the bottom of the sea and do not move about. Sometimes it is very difficult to say whether a thing is an animal or a plant. When you study botany, the science which deals with plants, or zoology, the science of animals, you will see these strange things which are neither wholly animal nor plant.

Some people tell us that even stones and rocks have some kind of life and that they feel a kind of pain. But it is difficult to see this. Perhaps you remember a gentleman who came to see us in Geneva. His name is Sir Jagadish Bose. He has shown by experiments that plants have a great deal of life, and he thinks that even stones have some life.

So you see it is not easy to say what thing is living and what is not. But let us leave out stones for the present and consider only plants and animals. We have today a vast number of living things. They are of all kinds. There are men and women, and some of them are very clever and some are fools. Then there are animals and among them too you find clever animals like the elephant or monkey or ant; you find also animals who are very stupid. Fishes and many other things in the seas are lower down still in the order of life. And right at the bottom of this order you find sponges and jelly-like fishes and those things which are half animal and half plants.

We have to try to find if all these different kinds of animals suddenly came into existence at one and the same time or gradually one by one. How are we to find this? We have no regular books of those ancient times. But can our book of nature help us? It does help. We find in the old rocks bones of animals. These are called fossils, and when we find them we can say that when that rock was formed long, long ago, the animals whose bones we have found must have lived. You saw many fossils of this kind, big and small, at the South Kensington Museum in London.

When an animal dies, his soft and fleshy parts go bad very quickly but his bones remain for a very long time, and it is these bones that we find and which tell us something of those animals of far-off days. But suppose an animal has no bones like the jellyfish. It will leave nothing behind when it dies.

When we examine the rocks carefully and collect all the old fossil bones that we find, we can see that different kinds of animals lived at different periods. They did not all come together from nowhere. At first, there are very simple animals with shells—shellfish for instance. The beautiful shells you pick up at the seaside are all the bony coverings of animals who have died. Later, we find more complicated animals: snakes, enormous beasts bigger than our elephant, and birds and animals resembling those we have today. Last of all, we find remains of man. So it appears as if there was a certain order in the appearance of animals—at first the simplest animals, then a higher type of animal getting more and more complicated till we reach what is called now the highest type of animal—man. How the simple sponge and shellfish developed and changed and improved themselves so much is a most interesting study, and perhaps some day I shall tell you about it. But at present we are concerned with the first living things.

Probably the first living things when the earth cooled down were soft jelly-like substances without any shell or bones, living in the sea. We have no fossil remains of these because they had no bones and so we have to guess more or less. There are many jelly-like things like these in the sea even today. They are round but their shape is continually changing as there is no bone or shell. They are something like this:

You will notice the spot in the centre. It is called the nucleus and it is a kind of heart. These animals, or whatever they are, have a curious way of dividing and becoming two. They start getting thinner at one place and go on doing so till they break off into two jelly-like things and both of these are just like the original one. This division takes place after this fashion:

You will see that the nucleus or heart also divides and each part gets a bit of it. In this way these animals go on dividing and increasing.

Something of this kind must have been the first living thing on this earth of ours. What a simple and humble representative of life it was! There was nothing better or higher in the whole earth then. The real animals had not come and man was not to come for millions of years.

These jelly-like things were followed by seaweeds and shellfish and crabs and worms. Then came fishes. We know a lot about these as they had hard bony parts or shells and they left these for us to find, so long after them, and to study them. The shells were left in the mud on the sea-floor. They were covered up by fresh mud and sand and so were preserved carefully. The mud became hard because of the weight and pressure of the sand and mud on top of it. It became so hard that it became a rock. In this way rocks were formed at the bottom of the sea.

An earthquake or something else brought out the rock from under the sea and it became dry land. Then the dry rock was washed away by the rivers and by rain, and the shells which had been hidden in it for ages and ages came out. This is how we come across these shells or fossils, and after studying them find out what our earth was like in the old days before man came.

We shall consider in the next letter how these simple animals developed and became what they are today.

❐

The Animals Appear

We have seen that the first signs of life on our earth probably were simple little sea animals and water plants. They could only live in the water and if they came out and dried up, they must have died as the jellyfish dies today if it gets stranded on the beach and dries up. But in those days there must have been plenty of water and marshy land, much more so than we have today. Now those jellyfishes and other sea animals which had slightly tougher skins could stay a little longer on dry land than the others as they did not dry up so soon. So gradually the soft jellyfishes and everything else like them became fewer and fewer as they could not face dry land easily, and those with harder coverings became more and more. This is a very interesting thing to notice. It means that animals slowly fit themselves or adapt themselves to their surroundings. You have seen in the South Kensington Museum in London how birds and animals in winter, and in cold countries where there is a lot of ice, become white like snow; in tropical countries where there is a lot of green vegetation and trees they became green or some other bright colour. That is, they adapt themselves to their surroundings. They change their colour to protect themselves from their enemies as they cannot easily be seen if they are the same colour as their surroundings. They grow fur in cold countries to keep warm in the cold. So also the tiger is yellow and striped. It is like sunlight coming through the trees in the jungle. It is difficult to see the tiger in the thick jungle.

This very interesting fact that animals try to fit in with their surroundings is a very important thing. Of course, animals do not themselves try to change. But those which change and therefore fit in with their surroundings have a better chance of living. So they increase in numbers and the others do not. This explains so many things. It explains the simple animals slowly developing into higher kinds of animals, and maybe in millions of years developing into man. We cannot see the changes going on around us as they are slow and our lives are short. But nature goes on working and changing and making more perfect. It never stops or takes rest.

Now you remember that the world was getting cooler and was slowly drying up. As it became cooler, the climate changed and many other things changed. As the earth changed, so also slowly the animals changed and newer types of animals appeared. At first, we have only simple sea animals, then complicated sea animals. Later, as dry land increased, there came animals which lived both in water and on land, something like the crocodiles today or the frogs. These were followed by animals which lived entirely on land, and then there came birds which could fly in the air.

I have mentioned the frog. This is an interesting study as in its own life it shows us in a way how animals gradually changed from water animals to land animals. A frog at first is a fish, but later it becomes like a land animal and breathes with its lungs as all land animals do.

There were great forests in those early days when life started on land. The land must have been all swampy with thick jungles on it. These forests later on got covered up and with the pressure of a great deal of rock and earth they slowly changed to coal. You know that we get our coal from mines deep down in the earth. The coal mines are really old forests of those far-off days.

Among the first land animals were enormous snakes and lizards and crocodiles. Some of these were a hundred feet long. Imagine a snake or a lizard one hundred feet long! Do you remember seeing the fossils of these brutes in the museum in London?

Later came animals which are more like the animals we see today. These are called mammals because they suckle their young. These also were at first much bigger than they are today. The mammal which most resembles man is the monkey or rather the ape. People think therefore that man is descended from the ape. This means that as each animal gradually adapted himself to his surroundings and became better and better, so also man at first was only a better ape. Of course, he went on improving, or nature went on improving him, and now man thinks no end of himself.

He imagines himself so utterly different from the animals. But it is good to remember that we are cousins of the ape and the monkey, and even now many of us, I am afraid, behave like the monkeys do!

❒

The Coming of Man

We saw in our last letter how life came to the earth in very simple forms and slowly through millions of years evolved and became what it is today. We also noticed one very interesting and important rule in this evolution of life—animals are always trying to adapt themselves to their surroundings. In trying to do this, they have developed many new qualities and have become higher more complicated animals. We can see this change or progress in many ways. For instance, first of all there were animals without bones, but as these could not survive for long, they developed bones. The first bone they developed was the backbone. So we have a division of animals—the boneless ones and those with bones. Man and the animals you see about you have, of course, bones.

Then again, you find the simple animals like fishes laying eggs and leaving them. They lay thousands of eggs at a time but do not look after them. The mother does not care for her children at all. She simply leaves the eggs and never comes back to them. As there is no one to look after them, most of these eggs die and only a few of them develop into fishes. Is this not terrible waste? As we go up and examine the higher animals we find that their eggs or children are fewer but they look after them better.

The hen also lays eggs but she sits upon them and so hatches them, and when the little chicks come out she feeds them for some time. When they grow up, the mother does not care much for them.

There comes a great change in the higher animals—the mammals—about whom I said something in my last letter. These animals do not lay eggs but the mother keeps the egg inside her and gives birth to the fully developed baby animal, like dogs or cats or rabbits. And afterwards the mother suckles, or gives milk, to her young. The mother thus looks after her babies a great deal. Even here, however, you find that there is great deal of waste. The mother rabbit gives birth to a large number of baby rabbits every few months and many of these die. But a higher animal like the elephant only gives birth to one baby elephant and looks after the baby well.

So you will see that as animals develop they do not lay eggs but bear developed young ones like themselves, only smaller, and the higher animals usually give birth to one baby at a time. You will also notice that the higher animals have some affection for their young ones. Man is the highest animal and so you find that the mother and the father love and take care of their children a great deal.

In this way, man must have first developed from the lower animals. Probably the first men were hardly men like we know them today. They must have been half apes, half men, living rather like monkeys. Do you remember going with us to see a professor in Heidelberg in Germany? He showed us a little museum full of fossils and especially an old skull which he kept carefully locked up in a safe. The skull was supposed to belong to one of these earliest men. We now call him the Heidelberg man, simply because the skull was found buried near Heidelberg. Of course there was no Heidelberg or any other city in those days.

In those early days when the first men wandered about, it used to be very cold. It is called the Ice Age because there was so much ice. Glaciers, such as now exist near the North Pole, came right down to England and Germany. The men must have found it very difficult to live and they must have had a hard time. They would only live where there were no glaciers. We are told by scientists that at that time the Mediterranean was not a sea at all but one or two lakes. There was no Red Sea either. It was all land. Probably the greater part of India was an island and the sea existed in the Punjab and part of our provinces. Imagine all South India and Central India as one big island cut off from the Himalayas by the sea! You would then have to go to Mussoorie partly by a steamer!

Man, when he first came, must have been surrounded by many huge animals, and he must have lived in fear of them. Today man is master of the world and he makes the animals do what he likes. Some he tames, like the horse, the cow, the elephant, the dog, the cat and so many others. Some he eats; and some, like the lion and the tiger, he shoots for pleasure. But in those days he was not the master but a poor hunted creature himself, trying to keep away from the great beasts. Gradually, however, man raised himself and became more and more powerful till he became stronger than any animal. How did he do this? Not by physical strength for the elephant is much stronger than he is. It was by intelligence and brain power.

We can trace this growth of intelligence from the earliest days of man to the present day. Indeed, it is intelligence that separates man from the other animals. There is practically no difference between a man without any intelligence and an animal.

The first great discovery that man probably made was that of fire. We light a fire now by a match. But of course matches are quite recent things. In olden times fires were made by rubbing two flints against each other till a spark and this spark set fire to a piece of dry straw or some other dry thing. Fires sometimes occur by themselves in the forests, perhaps by the rubbing together of flints or something else. The animals were not clever enough to learn anything from this. But man was cleverer. He saw the use of fire. It kept him warm in the winter and frightened away his enemies, the big animals. So whenever a fire started, the men and women must have tried to keep it up by throwing dry leaves into it. They did not want it to go out. Slowly, they must have found out that they themselves could produce a spark and a fire by rubbing flints together. This was a great discovery for them and it gave them some power over the other animals. Man was then well on his way to the lordship of the world.

❐

The Early Men

We saw in our last letter that the chief difference between man and the other animals was the intelligence of man. This intelligence made him cleverer and stronger than enormous animals who would otherwise have destroyed him. As man's intelligence grew, so also grew his power. To begin with, man had no special weapons to fight his enemies. He could only throw stones at them. Then he began to make out of stone: axes, spears and many other things, including fine stone needles. We saw many of these stone weapons in the South Kensington Museum and also in the museum in Geneva.

The Ice Age, about which I said something in my last letter, slowly ended and the glaciers disappeared from Central Europe and Asia. As it became warmer, men spread out.

In those days there were no houses or other buildings. People lived in caves. There was no cultivation, that is working in the fields. Men ate fruits and nuts and the animals they killed. They had no bread or rice because they did not grow anything in the fields. They did not know cooking but perhaps they just heated the meat on the big fires they had. They had no cooking vessels or pots and pans.

One thing is very curious. These savage men knew how to draw. Of course they had no paper or pens or pencils or brushes. They simply had their stone needles and pointed instruments. With these they scratched or drew animals on the walls of caves. Some of their drawings are quite good but they are almost all profiles. You know that it is easier to draw profiles, and children usually draw in this way. As the caves must have been dark it is probable that they used some kind of simple lamp.

These men that we have described are called Palaeolithic men, or the men of the old Stone Age. That period is called the Stone Age because men made all their tools with stone. They did not know how to use the metals. Today most of your things are made of metals, specially iron. But iron or bronze was not known then, and so stone, which is much more difficult to work with, was used.

Before the Stone Age came to an end, the climate of the world changed greatly and became much warmer. The glaciers had gone far back to the Arctic Ocean, and in Central Asia and Europe great forests arose. Among these forests we find a new race of men living. These people were cleverer in many ways than the Palaeolithic men whom we have just described. But they still made their tools out of stone. These men also belonged to the Stone Age but it was the later Stone Age. They are called Neolithic men or men of the new Stone Age.

We find when examining these Neolithic men that great progress has been made. The intelligence of man is making him go ahead fast compared to the other animals. These

Neolithic men made the very great discovery of cultivation. They started tilling fields and growing their food there. This was a great thing for them. They could now get their food more easily instead of having to hunt animals all the time. They got more leisure, more time to rest and think. And the more leisure they had, the more progress they made in discovering new things and methods. They started making earthen pots, and with the help of these they began to cook their food. The stone tools were much better and were beautifully polished. They also knew how to tame animals like the cow, the dog, the sheep and the goat. They also knew how to weave.

They used to live in houses or huts. These huts were very often made in the middle of lakes as the wild animals or other men could not attack them easily there. These people are therefore called lake-dwellers.

You will wonder how we know so much about these people. They wrote no books of course. But I have already told you that the book where we read the story of these men is the great book of nature. It is not easy to read it. It requires great patience. Many people have spent their lives in trying to read this book and they have collected large numbers of fossils and other remains of old times. These fossils are collected together in the great museums, and we can see there the fine polished axes and the pots and stone arrows and needles and many other things which were made by the Neolithic man. You have seen many of these things yourself but perhaps you have forgotten them. If you see them again you will be able to understand them better.

There was, I remember, a very good model of a lake-dwelling in the Geneva museum. Wooden poles were stuck in the lake, and on top of these poles a wooden platform was made. On the platform the wooden huts were put up and the thing was connected by a little bridge to the land.

These Neolithic men clothed themselves with the skins of animals or sometimes with a rough cloth of flax. Flax is a plant which has a good fibre used for making cloth. Linen is now made out of flax. But in those days cloth of flax must have been very rough.

These men went on making progress. They started making tools of copper and of bronze. Bronze, as you know, is a mixture of copper and tin and is harder than either of these. They also used gold and were vain enough to make ornaments out of it!

These people must have lived about 10,000 years ago. Of course, we do not know the exact dates or periods. All this is largely guesswork. You will notice that so far we have been talking of millions of years. We are now gradually getting nearer and nearer to our present age. From the Neolithic man to the man today there is no break or sudden change. But still we are very different from him. The changes came slowly, as is nature's way. Different races developed and each race went its own way and lived its own life. The climate being different in different parts of the world, people had to adapt themselves to it and changed greatly. But we shall talk about this later.

One thing more I want to tell you today. About the end of the Neolithic age a very great disaster happened to man. I have told you already that at that time the Mediterranean was not a sea at all. There were just some lakes there and in these lakes many people lived. Suddenly, the land near Gibraltar, between Europe and Africa, was washed away and the waters of the Atlantic Ocean poured into the low valley of the Mediterranean. The water went on pouring and filling it up, and large numbers of the men and women living near or over the lakes must have been drowned. They could not escape anywhere. There was water all over the place for hundreds of miles. The Atlantic Ocean continued to pour in till it had filled up the valley, and the Mediterranean Sea came into existence.

You have heard, of course, and perhaps read, about the great flood. The Bible speaks about it and some of our Sanskrit books also refer to it. It may be that this mighty flood was the filling up of the Mediterranean. It was such a terrible disaster that the few people who managed to escape must have told all about it to their children, and they to their own children, and so the story was handed down from generation to generation.

❐

How Different Races Were Formed

We discussed in our last letter the Neolithic men who used to live chiefly in lake dwellings. We saw that they had made great progress in many ways. They discovered agriculture and knew how to cook and to tame animals for their use. All this was many thousands of years ago and we do not know much about them. But probably most of the races of men we have in the world today have descended from these Neolithic people. We find now, as you know, white men and yellow men and brown and black. But as a matter of fact, it is not easy to divide the races of men into these four divisions. Races have got mixed up and it is difficult to say about many of them to which division they belong. Scientists measure the heads of people and by this measurement they can sometimes find out the race. There are other ways of finding this out also.

How did these different races come into existence? If they are all descended from the same people, why do they differ so much from each other now? You know that a German is very different from a Negro. One is fair and the other is black. The hair of the German is light coloured and long, the Negro's hair is black and short and curly. The

Chinaman again is different from both of these. It is difficult to say how these differences crept in, but we know some of the causes of these differences. I have already told you how animals gradually changed as they adapted themselves to their surroundings. It may be that the German and the Negro are descended from different types of men, but some time or other they must have had the same ancestor. The differences must therefore have come in by the process of adaption to their surroundings, or it may have been that some, like some animals, could adapt themselves more easily than others.

Thus a person living in the great cold and ice of the far north would develop the power to bear cold. The Eskimos even now live in the ice fields of the north and they can bear great cold. They would probably die if you brought them to warm countries like ours. And as they are cut off from the rest of the world, and have to live a hard life, they have not learnt as many things as people in other parts of the world.

The people in Africa or those living near the equator where it is very hot, get used to this heat. And the great heat of the sun makes them dark in complexion. You know that if you spend much time in the sun at the seaside or elsewhere, you become tanned, or browner and darker than you otherwise are. If after a few weeks of sunbaths you become darker, how much darker would a man be who always has to live in this sun? And if for hundreds of years people live in very hot countries, fathers and their children and their children's children and so on, they will become darker and darker, till they become almost black. You have seen the Indian peasant working in the fields in the midday sun. He is too poor to have many clothes and has little on. His whole body is exposed to the sun and all his life is spent in this way. He is bound to get dark.

So we find that people's complexions are the result of the climate they live in. They have nothing to do with the worthiness or goodness or beauty of a person. A white person living long in a hot country will get dark unless of course he hides himself from the sun and the heat behind *tattis* and under fans. You know we are Kashmiris and more than 200 years ago our ancestors lived in Kashmir. In Kashmir you find everybody, including the peasants and labourers, very fair of complexion. That is beacause the climate of Kashmir is cold. But these very Kashmiris when they come down to other parts of India, which are hotter, become darker after some generations. Many of our Kashmiri friends are quite fair, others are quite dark. The longer a Kashmiri family has lived in this part of India, the darker it is likely to be.

Climate is thus the chief cause of colour and complexion. Of course, it may be that some people, even though they may live in a hot country, do not work in the open and are rich enough to live in big houses and take care of themselves and their complexions. A rich family may live like this for generations and may thus not be affected by the climate very much. But not to work oneself and to live on the work of others is nothing to be proud of.

In India, you find that in the north, in Kashmir and Punjab, people are usually fair. But as you go south they become darker. In Madras and Ceylon, as you saw, they are quite dark. Of course you will say that this is due to the climate for as you go south you go nearer to the equator and it becomes hotter. This is quite true and is the principal reason for the difference of colour in various parts of India. We shall see, however, later that this difference is partly also due to some difference in the original races which came to India. Many races have come to India in past ages and although for long they tried to keep apart, they could not help mixing together. It is difficult now to say that a particular Indian belongs entirely to one original race.

❐

The Races and Languages of Mankind

We cannot say in what part of the world man first came into existence, nor do we know where the first human settlements were. Perhaps men came into existence in several parts at more or less the same time. It is likely, however, that when the great glaciers of the Ice Age were melting away and going back towards the north, men lived in the warmer regions. When the ice went, there must have been vast steppes, something like the tundras which we have in Siberia now. These must have become grasslands, and men must have wandered about them as they wanted grass for their cattle. These people who have no fixed place to live in and are always wandering about are called 'nomads'. Even now, we have some nomads in many countries, including India, like the gypsies.

People must have settled down near great rivers, for the land near the rivers was very rich and good for agriculture. There was plenty of water and it was easy to grow food on the land. So we suppose that people settled in India near the great rivers like the Indus and Ganges; and in Mesopotamia near the rivers Tigris and Euphrates; and in Egypt near the river Nile; and so also in China.

In India, the earliest race about which we know anything is the Dravidian race. Later, as we shall see, the Aryans came, and the Mongolians in the East. Even now most of the people living in South India are descended from the Dravidians. They are darker in colour than the northern people because perhaps the Dravidians have been much longer in India. The Dravidians were very advanced people and had their own languages and carried on a lot of business with other people. But we are going too fast ahead.

In those early days, a new race was developing in Central and Western Asia and in Eastern Europe. This is called the Aryan race. In Sanskrit there is the same word आर्य (Arya), meaning a gentleman or a high-born person. As Sanskrit was one of the languages of the Aryan peoples, this means that they considered themselves very gentlemanly and high-born! They were apparently quite as vain as people are now. You know that an Englishman thinks himself quite the first person on earth, and a Frenchman is equally sure that the French are the greatest people, so also the German and the American and others.

These Aryans wandered about Northern Asia and Europe over the wide grasslands. But as their numbers grew and the climate became drier and the land grassless, there was not enough food for all of them to eat. So they were forced to move to other parts of the world in search of food. They spread out all over Europe and came to India and Persia and Mesopotamia. Thus we find that nearly all the peoples of Europe and Northern India and Persia and Mesopotamia, although they differ so much from each other now, are really descended from the same ancestors—the Aryans. Of course, this was very long ago and since then much has happened and races have got mixed up to a large extent. The Aryans are therefore one great ancestor race of the peoples of the world today.

Another great race is the Mongolian. This spread out all over Eastern Asia—in China and Japan and Tibet, Siam and Burma. They are sometimes called the yellow race and you will find that they usually have high cheek bones and narrow eyes.

The people of Africa and some other places are the Negroes. They are neither Aryans nor Mongolians, and are very dark in colour.

The peoples of Arabia and Palestine—the Arabs and Hebrews—belong to yet a different race.

All these races have, in the course of thousands of years, split up into many smaller races and got a little mixed up, but we need not trouble ourselves about these. An important and interesting way of distinguishing between different races is by studying their languages. Each race had originally a separate language, but in the course of time, many languages developed from this one language. But all these languages were the children of one parent language and belong to the same family. We can easily spot common words in them and see the connexion between different languages.

When the Aryans spread out over Asia and Europe, they could not remain in touch with each other. In those days there were no railways or telegraphs or posts or even written books. So each group of Aryans began to speak the same language, each in its own way, and after some time this became quite different from the parent language or from its cousins in other Aryan countries.

For this reason we now find so many languages in the world.

We shall find, however, if we study these languages that although they are so many, the parent languages are few. For instance, wherever the Aryans went the language belonged to the Aryan family. Sanskrit and Latin and Greek and English, French, German, Italian and some other languages are all cousins and belong to the Aryan family. Many of our Indian languages like Hindi, Urdu, Bengali, Marathi and Gujarati are all children of Sanskrit and so they also belong to the Aryan family.

Another big language family is the Chinese. This has Chinese, Burmese, Tibetan and Siamese.

A third group is the Semitic, which includes Arabic and Hebrew.

Some languages like Turkish and Japanese do not fall into any of these three groups. Some of the languages of South India, like Tamil and Telugu and Malayalam and Canarese also do not belong to these groups. These four are of the Dravidian family and are very old.

❐

The Relationships of Languages

We have seen how the Aryans spread out over many countries, and carried their language, whatever it was, wherever they went. But different climates and different conditions produced many differences in various groups of the Aryans. Each group went on changing in its own way with new habits and customs. They could not meet the other groups in other countries as it was exceedingly difficult to travel about in those days. Each group was cut off from the others. If the people of one country learnt something new, they could not tell it to the people of another country. So changes came in, and after some generations the one Aryan family became split up into many. Perhaps they even forgot that they all belonged to one large family. Their one language became many languages, which seemed to differ greatly from each other.

But although they seemed so different there were many common words and similarities. Even now, after thousands of years, we can find these common words in different languages and can tell that once upon a time these languages must have been one. You know that there are many such common words in French and English. Let us examine two homely and ordinary words like ‘father’ and ‘mother’. In Hindi and Sanskrit, the words are, as you know, पिता and माता; in Latin they are ‘pater’ and ‘mater’, in Greek ‘pater’ and ‘meter’; in German ‘vater’ (pronounced फातर), and ‘mutter’ (pronounced मुतर); in French ‘pere’ and ‘mere’; and so on in many other languages. Do they not all seem to be very much alike? They have a family resemblance, like cousins. Many words, of course, may be borrowed by one language from another. Hindi has borrowed many words from English in this way, and English has borrowed some words from Hindi. But ‘father’ and ‘mother’ could not have been borrowed. They cannot be new words. Right at the beginning, when people started talking to each other, there were of course fathers and mothers and words must have been found for them. Therefore, we can say that these words are not borrowed. They must have come down from the same ancestor or the same family. And from this we can find out that the people living far apart now in different countries and using different languages must have belonged once upon a time to the same big family.

You will see how interesting the study of language is and what a lot it teaches us. If we know three or four languages, it is not very difficult to learn more languages.

You will also see that most of us now living in different countries far from each other long ago were one people. We have changed greatly since then and many of us have forgotten our old relationships. In every country people imagine that they are the best and the cleverest and the others are not as good as they are. The Englishman thinks that he and his country are the best; the Frenchman is very proud of France and everything French; the Germans and Italians think no end of their countries; and many Indians imagine that India is in many ways the greatest country in the world. This is all conceit. Everybody wants to think well of himself and his country. But really there is no person who has not got some good in him and some bad. And in the same way there is no country which is not partly good and partly bad. We must take the good wherever we find it and try to remove the bad wherever it may be.

We are, of course, most concerned with our own country, India. Unhappily it is in a bad way today and most of our people are very poor and miserable. They have no pleasure in their lives. We have to find out how we can make them happier. We have to see what is good in our ways and customs and try to keep it, and whatever is bad, we have to throw away. If we find anything good in other countries, we should certainly take it.

As Indians we have to live in India and work for India. But we must not forget that we belong to the larger family of the world and the people living in other countries are after all our cousins. It would be such an excellent thing if all the people in the world were happy and contented. We have therefore to try to make the whole world a happier place to live in.

❐

What is Civilization?

I am going to tell you something about the early civilizations. But before I do so, we must try to form some idea of what civilization means. The dictionary will tell you that to civilize means to better, to refine, to replace savage habits by good ones. And it especially refers to society or a group of people. The savage condition of people when men are little better than beasts is called barbarism. Civilization is the reverse of that. The further away we get from barbarism, the more civilized we are.

But how can we find out if a person or a society is barbarous or civilized? Many people in Europe think that they are very civilized and the people of Asia are quite barbarous. Is this because the people of Europe put on more clothes than the peoples of Asia and Africa? But clothes depend on the climate. In a cold climate men put on more clothes than in a hot climate. Or is it because a man with a gun is stronger than the man without a weapon and is therefore more civilized than him? Whether he is more civilized or not, the man who is weak dare not tell him that he is not or else he might get shot!

You know that only a few years ago there was a great war. Most of the countries of the world were in it, and every one of them was trying to kill as many people on the other side as possible. The Englishman was trying his best to kill Germans. And the Germans were killing Englishmen. Millions of people were killed in this war and many thousands were maimed for life—some have no eyes left and are blind, others have no arms or legs. You must have seen many of these '*mutil'es de la guerre*', war-wounded people, in France and elsewhere. In the Paris underground railway, the Metro, there are special seats for them.

Do you think it was a very civilized or sensible thing for people to kill each other like this? If two men fight in the streets the policeman separates them and everybody thinks how silly they are. But how much sillier and more foolish it is for great countries to fight each other and kill thousands and millions. It is just like two savages fighting in the jungles. And if the savages are called barbarous, how much more barbarous are the countries that behave in that way?

So if you look at this question in this way you will say that the countries that fought and killed in the Great War—England, Germany, France, Italy and many others—are not at all civilized. And yet you know that there are many fine things and many fine people in these countries.

You will say that it is not easy to understand what civilization means, and you will be right. It is a very difficult question. Fine buildings, fine pictures and books and everything that is beautiful are certainly signs of civilization. But an even better sign is a fine man who is unselfish and works with others for the good of all. To work together is better than to work singly, and to work together for the common good is the best of all.

❒

The Formation of Tribes

I have told you in my previous letters how man was very much like an animal when he first appeared on the earth. Slowly, over thousands of years, he developed and became something better. At first he must have hunted all by himself, like some of the wild beasts today. Then he found that it was wiser and safer to go about in herds with other men. If many men kept together, they were stronger and could defend themselves better against the attacks of beasts and maybe of other men. Even the animals go about in herds in this way for their own safety. Sheep and goats and deer and even elephants move about in herds. When the herds sleep, some of them remain awake and watch over them. You must have read stories of packs of wolves also. In Russia, in winter, these wolves go about in packs and when they are hungry, as they often are in winter, they attack men. One wolf would seldom attack a man, but a crowd of them feel strong enough to attack a party of men. And the men have to fly for their lives, and often there is a race between the wolves and the men on sledges on the ice.

So also the first advance in civilization that early men made was to combine together in packs or, as these are called, tribes. They began to work together. There was what is called cooperation. Each man had to think of the tribe first and then about himself. If the tribe was in danger every member of it had to fight for it and defend it. And if any person in the tribe did not work for the tribe, he was kicked out.

Now if people work together, they must act in an orderly way. If everyone were to do just what he pleased there would not be much of the tribe left. So someone has to become the leader. Even the herds of animals have leaders. The tribes of men also chose the strongest man amongst them as their leader. As there was a great deal of fighting to be done, the strongest man was chosen.

If the members of the tribes fought amongst themselves the tribe would soon break up. So the leader saw to it that fighting within the tribe was not allowed. Of course, one tribe could and did fight another. This was an improvement on the old method of each person fighting everybody else for himself.

The first tribes must really have been large families. All the members of them were related to each other. But the families grew and grew till the tribe became quite big.

It must have been a hard life to live for man in the early days, specially before tribes were formed. He had no house, no clothes except perhaps some skins, and he must have been continually fighting. To get his daily food he had to hunt and kill animals or gather nuts and fruits. He must have felt that he had enemies everywhere. Even nature must have seemed to him an enemy, sending hail and snow and earthquakes. Poor little slave he was, creeping about the earth, afraid of everything because he could understand nothing. If the hail came he thought that some god in the clouds was trying to hit him. And he became frightened and wanted to do something to please this person in the clouds who sent the hail and the rain and the snow. How could he please him? He was not very clear or brainy. He must have thought that the god in the clouds was like himself and liked food. So he would take some meat or kill an animal, sacrifice it as they say, and leave it somewhere for the god to eat! He imagined that he could stop the rain or the hail like this!

This seems very silly to us as we know why rain comes or hail or snow. The killing of an animal has nothing to do with it. But silly as it is, there are many people even today who are ignorant enough to do such things.

❒

How Religion Began and Division of Labour

In the last letter, I told you how the early men werc afraid of everything and imagined that every misfortune was caused by angry and jealous gods. They saw these imaginary gods everywhere—in the jungle, in the mountains, in the river, in the clouds. Their idea of god was not of a kind and good person but of a very irritable person who was always losing his temper. And as they were afraid of his anger they were always trying to bribe him by giving him something, chiefly food. Sometimes if a disaster came, like an earthquake or a flood or disease which killed large numbers of people, they would become very frightened and think that the gods were angry. And to please them they would go so far as to sacrifice men and women, even kill their own children, and offer them to the gods. This seems horrible but a man who is afraid will do anything.

This must have been the beginning of religion. So religion first came as fear, and anything that is done because of fear is bad. Religion, as you know, tells us many beautiful things. When you grow up, you will read about the religions of the world and of the good things and the bad things that have been done in their name. It is interesting to notice here, however, how the idea of religion began. Later we shall see how it grew. But however much it may have grown, we see even today that people fight and break each other's heads in the name of religion. And for many people it is still something to be afraid of. They spend their time in trying to please some imaginary beings by making presents in temples and even sacrifices of animals.

So early man had a hard life. He had to get his food almost daily or else he starved. No idle man could live in those days. It was not possible for anyone even to get together a lot of food and then do nothing for a long time.

When the tribe was formed, it became a little easier for man. All the members of the tribe working together could get more food than each one singly could have done. You know that working together or cooperation helps us to do many things which we cannot do singly. One man or two may not be able to carry a heavy load, but several men helping each other can easily do so. Another great advance came in those days about which I have already told you. This was agriculture. You will be interested to know that there are the beginnings of agriculture among some ants. Of course, I do not mean to say that ants sow seeds and plough and then reap the harvest. But what these ants do is something like this: if they find a shrub the seeds of which they eat, they take out the grass carefully from around the herb. This gives the herb a greater chance to live.

Perhaps men also did at one time what these ants do. They did not then understand what agriculture was. It must have taken them long ages to understand it and to begin to sow seeds.

With the coming of agriculture, it was much easier to get food. Men did not have to hunt all the time for it. So they could live a less hard life than they used to. Another interesting change now took place. Before agriculture, every man was a hunter. That was the only work to be done by the men. The women probably looked after the children and gathered fruit. But when agriculture came there were different kinds of work. There was work in the fields and hunting and looking after the cattle. Probably the women looked after the cattle and milked the cows. Some men did one kind of work, others another kind of work.

You find today in the world each person doing one particular kind of work. A man is a doctor, or an engineer, building bridges and roads, or a carpenter, or a blacksmith, or a mason who builds houses, or a shoemaker or a tailor, and so on. Each man has got his special trade and does not know much or anything of other trades. This is called division of work or division of labour. If a man tries to do one thing well, he will do it much better than if he tried to do many things. There is a great deal of division of labour in the world today.

We see this division of labour slowly beginning in the old tribes when agriculture came in.

❐

The Changes Brought about by Agriculture

In my last letter, I told you something about the division of labour. Right at the beginning, when men used to live by hunting only, there was very little division of work. Everybody hunted and they could, with difficulty, get enough to eat. The division of work or labour must have begun between men and women—the men hunting and the women staying at home and looking after the children and domestic animals.

When people learnt about agriculture, many new developments took place. There was, firstly, a greater division of labour. Some people hunted, others looked after the fields and ploughed. Then again, as the time went on, people learnt new trades and specialized in them.

Another interesting result of tilling land was that men began to settle down in villages and towns. Before agriculture came, people used to wander about and hunt. It was not necessary for them to live in one place. They could hunt wherever they went. And often they had to move about from place to place because of the cows and sheep and other animals they had. These animals required pasture lands where they could graze. After grazing in one place for some time, the land did not produce enough for the cattle, and so the whole tribe had to move to another place.

When agriculture came, people had to stay near the land. They could not leave the land they had ploughed and sowed. And so they worked there from harvest to harvest, and villages and towns grew up.

Another great change that agriculture brought about was to make life easier. It was far simpler to grow food on the land by agriculture than to hunt all the time. The land also gave more food than could be eaten up at once. This was kept carefully.

Now let us note an interesting development. When man was a hunter pure and simple, he could not hoard anything or at any rate very little. He had to live, as they say, from hand to mouth. He had no banks where he could keep his money or other goods. He had to earn his food every day by hunting. With the coming of agriculture, he got more from the land at one time than could be used. He hoarded up this surplus or extra food. Here we find the beginnings of surplus food. People got this surplus food because they worked a little more than was quite necessary for them to produce just sufficient food.

You know that now we have banks and people deposit money there and draw it out by cheques. Where does this money come from? If you think about it, you will see that this money is all surplus, that is people do not want to spend it all at one time and so they keep it in banks. The rich people today are those who have plenty of this surplus, the poor have none at all. Later, you will see how this surplus comes. It is not so much because one person works more than another, but nowadays a person who does not work at all gets the surplus, while the hard worker often gets no part of it! This seems a very silly arrangement. Many people think that it is because of this stupid arrangement that there are so many poor people in the world. This may seem a little difficult for you to understand now. If so, do not trouble yourself about it. You will understand it soon enough.

At present I should only like you to note that agriculture resulted in producing much more than could be eaten up at once. This was hoarded up. In those days there were no banks or money. People were called rich who had many cows or sheep or camels.

❒

The Patriarch — How He Began

I am afraid my letters are getting a little complicated! But the life we see around us is itself very complicated. In the old days it was much simpler, but we are now considering the time when complications first began. If we follow up our inquiry slowly, and try to understand the changes in life and society as they came in, we shall find it easier to understand many things today. And if we do not try to do so, we shall never be able to understand all that is happening around us. We shall be like children lost in a dark forest. It is for this reason that I am trying to take you right back to the edge of the forest so that we may be able to find a way through it.

You will remember that you asked me in Mussoorie about kings, and what they were, and why they became kings. We are now going to have a little peep in those far-off days when kings began. They were not called kings to begin with. But if we try to find out something about them, we shall know the origin of kings.

I have told you already about the formation of tribes. When agriculture came, and there was some division of work or labour, it became necessary for some person in the tribe to organize the work. Even before this, the tribes wanted someone to lead them to battle against another tribe. The leader was usually the oldest man in the group. He was called, or rather we call him now, the patriarch. As the oldest, he was supposed to be the most experienced and to have the most knowledge. This patriarch was not very different from the other members of the tribe. He worked with the others, and all the food that was produced was divided between all the members of the tribe. Everything belonged to the tribe. It was not like we have now, each person having his separate house and money and many other things. Whatever a man earned was divided up as it all belonged to the tribe. The patriarch or the organizer of the tribe did this dividing.

But changes came in slowly. There were new kinds of work, especially on account of agriculture, and the patriarch had to spend most of his time in organizing, and seeing that work was properly done by all the members of the tribe. Little by little, the patriarch gave up doing the ordinary work or labour of the people. He thus became quite different from the rest of the people. We see now another kind of division of work or labour: the patriarch doing the organizing and ordering people about, and the other people working in the fields and hunting and going to battle, and obeying the orders of their leader, the patriarch. If there was a war or a fight between two tribes, the patriarch became even more powerful, for in wartime it was not possible to fight well without a leader. So the patriarch became very powerful.

As the work of organizing increased, the patriarch could not do it all by himself. He chose other people to help him. So we have many organizers, but of course the patriarch was the chief. The tribe was then divided up into organizers and ordinary workers. Men were no longer more or less equal. Some men, who were the organizers, had power over the other men, who were the ordinary workers. We shall see how the patriarch developed in our next letter.

❐

The Patriarch — How He Developed

I hope you do not find my account of the old tribes and their patriarchs very dull. I told you in my last letter that everything in those days belonged to the whole tribe and not to each member separately. Even the patriarch had nothing special to himself. As a member of the tribe, he could only have a share like any other member. But he was the organizer and he was supposed to look after the goods and property of the tribe. As his power increased, he began to think that these goods and property were really his own and not the tribe's. Or rather he thought that he himself, being the leader of the tribe, represented the tribe. So we see how the idea of owning things for oneself began. Today we are always thinking and talking of this thing being 'mine' or 'yours'. But, as I have told you, the men and women of the first tribes did not think in this way. Everything then belonged to the tribe.

The old patriarch, however, began to think that he was the tribe, and so he looked upon most of the things belonging to the tribe as his own.

When the patriarch died, all the members of the tribe gathered together and chose another person to be their leader or patriarch. But usually the family of the patriarch knew more about the work of organization than the others. As they were always with the patriarch, they used to help him in his work and so they got to know about it. It so happened therefore that when an old patriarch died, the members of the tribe chose someone else from the same family. So we find that the patriarch's family became different from the others and the tribe always chose its leaders from this family. Now the patriarch had a great deal of power. Naturally, he wanted his own son or brother to succeed him as patriarch and he tried his best to bring this about. So he trained his son or brother or some other near relative so that he might succeed him. He even told the tribe that a certain person whom he had selected and trained must become patriarch after him. Perhaps to begin with, the members of the tribe did not like being told so, but they soon got used to it and always did what the patriarch wanted them to do. There was practically no election or choosing of a new patriarch. The old man had already decided who was to be his successor and this man succeeded.

So we see that the office of the patriarch became hereditary, that is, it remained in the same family and went from father to son or some other relative. The patriarch now was quite sure that the property and things belonging to the tribe were really his own. Even when he died they remained in his family. We see how the idea of anything belonging to 'me' or 'you' started. There was no such idea to begin with. People all worked together for the tribe and not for themselves. If they produced a lot of food or other things, everybody in the tribe got his share. There were no rich or poor in the tribe. They were all sharers in the property of the tribe.

But as soon as the patriarch started grabbing at the things belonging to the tribe and calling them his own, we begin to get rich people and poor people.

I shall have something more to say about this in my next letter.

❐

The Patriarch Becomes the King

The old patriarch has taken up a lot of our time, has he not? We shall finish with him soon, or rather he will change his name. I started by promising to tell you how kings came and what they were. And in order to understand kings one has to go right back to the patriarchs. You must have guessed that these patriarchs became later on kings or raja and maharaja. The word patriarch comes from the Latin 'Pater' or father. He was the leader and father of his tribe or people. 'Patria', which means fatherland or one's own country, comes from the same Latin word. You know that in French it is 'Patrie'. In Sanskrit and Hindi, we think of our country as the mother or motherland—*Matribhumi*, the motherland. Which do you prefer?

When the patriarch's office became hereditary, that is son succeeded father, there was little difference between him and a king. He developed into a king and the king got the strange notion that everything in the country belonged to him. He thought he was the country. A famous French king once said *L'etat c'est moi*— 'The State, it is I' or 'I am the state'. Kings forgot that they were really chosen by the people in order to organize and distribute the food and other things of the country among the people. They forgot that they were chosen because they were supposed to be the cleverest and the most experienced persons in the tribe or country. They imagined that they were the masters and all the other people in the country their servants. As a matter of fact, they were the servants of the country.

Later on, you will see when you read history that kings became so conceited that they thought that the people had nothing to do with choosing them. It was God himself, they said, that had made them kings. They called this the 'divine right of kings'. For long years, they misbehaved like this and lived in great pomp and luxury while their people starved. But, at last, the common people could not bear it any longer and in some countries they drove out their kings. You will read all about this later, how the people of England rose against their King Charles I and defeated him and even put him to death; how the people of France had a great revolution and decided to have no more kings. You will remember that we visited the Conciergerie prison in Paris. Were you with us then? In this prison were kept the members of the king's family, his wife Marie Antoinette and others. You will also read about the great Russian revolution when the people of Russia, only a few years ago, drove out their king, who was called the Tsar.

So kings have had their day and most countries have no kings. France and Germany and Russia and Switzerland and the countries of America and China and many other countries have no kings. They are republics, that is, the common people choose their governors and leaders from time to time. These governors and leaders are not hereditary.

In England, as you know, there is still a king, but he has no power. He can do very little. All the power belongs to the Parliament, where the chosen leaders of the people sit. You will remember seeing the Parliament in London.

In India, we have still many rajas and maharajas and nawabs. You see them going about with fine clothes, in expensive motor cars and spending a lot of money on themselves. Where do they get all this money from? They get it in taxes from the people. The taxes are given so that the money may be used to help all the people in the country—by making schools and hospitals and libraries and museums and good roads and many other things for the good of the people. But our rajas and maharajas still think as the French king did of old: *L'etat c'est moi*—The State, it is I. And they spend the money of the people on their own pleasures. While they live in luxury, their people, who work hard and give them the money, starve and their children have no schools to go to.

❐

The Early Civilization

We have said enough about patriarchs and kings for the time being. Let us now go back a little and consider the early civilizations and the kind of people who lived in those days.

We do not know very much about these early peoples, but we know much more about them than about the Palaeolithic and Neolithic man. We have got even now huge buildings in ruins which were built thousands of years ago. And looking at these buildings and temples and palaces, we can form some idea of what the early people were like and what they did. Specially helpful to us are the sculptures and carvings in these old buildings. From these sculptures we can find out sometimes what kind of dress they used to wear and many other things.

We cannot say definitely where men first settled down and developed a civilization. Some people say that there was a great country, which they now call Atlantis, in the Atlantic Ocean. In this country, it is said, people lived and were highly civilized, but the whole country somehow or other was swallowed up by the Atlantic Ocean and no part of it remains. We have no proof of this, only stories. So we can leave this out and need not consider it.

Then again we are told by some people that there were great civilizations in olden times in America. You know that Columbus is supposed to have discovered America. But this does not mean that America was not there before Columbus came. It simply means that the people of Europe did not know of it till Columbus found it out for them. Long before Columbus went there, people lived there and had some kind of civilization. We find ruins of very old buildings in Yukatan, which is in Mexico in North America, and in Peru in South America. We can certainly say therefore that in Peru and Yukatan civilized people lived in very early times. But we cannot say much more about them, as we do not know much at present. Perhaps we may find out many more facts about them later.

In Eurasia, as Europe and Asia together are called, the earliest civilizations were probably in Mesopotamia, Egypt, Crete, India and China. Egypt is now considered to be in Africa, but we may consider it with Eurasia as it is very near.

When the old tribes which used to wander about wanted to settle down, what kind of place would they choose? It must be a place where they could get their food easily; and their food was partly grown in the fields by agriculture. For agriculture, water is very necessary. Without water, the fields dry up and nothing can be grown in them. You know that when there is not enough rain during the monsoon in India, little food is grown and there is a famine. The poor get nothing to eat and starve. So water is essential. The early settlers must therefore have chosen places to live in where there was plenty of water. We find that this was so.

In Mesopotamia, they settled down between the two great rivers, the Tigris and the Euphrates. In Egypt, they had the great Nile. In India, most of their cities were near the big rivers—the Indus, the Ganges, the Jumna. Water was so necessary for them that they looked upon those rivers which gave them food and abundance, as sacred and holy. In Egypt, they called the Nile 'Father Nile', and worshipped it. In India, you know that the Ganges was worshipped and is still considered holy. It is called 'Mother Ganges' (Ganga mai) and you hear pilgrims shout out 'Ganga *mai ki-jai*'. It is quite easy to understand this worship as these rivers meant so much to them. They gave them not only water but fine mud and sand which made the fields rich and fertile. Because of the river water and mud, the land gave plenty of food. So the rivers might well be called 'father' and 'mother'. But people have a habit of forgetting why they do things. Unthinkingly, they go on copying others. We must remember that the Nile and the Ganges are considered holy because they gave water and food.

❒

The Great Cities of the Ancient World

We have seen that people first settled down near big rivers and in fertile valleys where food and water were abundant. Their big cities were on the banks of the rivers. You may have heard the names of some of these famous old cities. In Mesopotamia, there were Babylon and Nineveh and Assur. But all of these have long ceased to exist and people sometimes find remains of the cities if they dig deep enough in the sand or earth. In thousands of years, they were covered up completely by sand and earth and no trace of them could be seen. In some places, new cities were built right on top of the old ones which were covered up. People who have been trying to find out about these old cities have had to dig deep, and sometimes they have found several cities one on top of the other. Of course, they did not exist like this at the same time. One city probably existed for hundreds of years and people lived in it and died, and their children and children's children lived and died. Gradually, the city became deserted and fewer people lived in it. At last, nobody lived there and the whole place became a heap of ruins. The sand and the dust came and covered up these cities and there was no one to remove it. After many, many years the whole city became covered up with this sand and dust and people even forgot that the city ever existed. Hundreds of years must have passed, and then fresh people came there and built a new city. And this new city in its turn became old and deserted and fell into ruins. And that too disappeared in the course of time under sand and dust. So we find sometimes the ruins of many cities one over the other. This happened specially in sandy places for the sand covers everything quickly.

Strange, is it not, that city after city should grow up and shelter crowds of men and women and children, and then gradually die away? And new cities grow where the old used to be and fresh crowds of people come and live in them. And they too die and leave no sign or trace behind. I write about these cities in a few sentences, but think of the thousands and thousands of years that must have passed for these cities to grow and die, and other cities to take their place. We call a man old when he is seventy or eighty years of age. But what is seventy or eighty when we think of these thousands of years? How many little children must have become old and died again and again in these cities when they existed. And now Babylon and Nineveh are but names for us.

Another very old city was Damascus in Syria. But Damascus did not die. It is still there and is a great city. It is said by some that Damascus is probably the oldest city in the world today.

In India, our great cities are also on the banks of rivers. One of the oldest was Indraprastha, which was somewhere near Delhi. But Indraprastha is no more. Benares or Kashi is also very old, perhaps one of the oldest existing cities of the world. Allahabad, Kanpur and Patna, and many others which you can probably yourself think of, are also on the banks of rivers. But these are not very old, though Prayag or Allahabad and Patna or Pataliputra, as it used to be called, are pretty old.

So also there are ancient cities in China.

❐

Egypt and Crete

What kind of people lived in these cities and villages of early times? We can find something about them from the great buildings and structures that they made. Also from the writing on stone tablets which they left. Then we have a few very old books which tell us a great deal of those times.

In Egypt we still have the great pyramids and the Sphinx and ruins of enormous temples at Luxor and other places. You have not seen these although we were not far from them when we passed through the Suez Canal. But you have seen pictures of them and probably you have got picture postcards of them. The Sphinx is a lion with a woman's head. It is an enormous thing. Nobody knows why it was made and what it represents. The woman's head has got a strange faint smile and people wonder what this smile is about. To say that a person is like the Sphinx means that you do not understand him.

The pyramids are also enormous structures. They are really the tombs of the old kings of Egypt who were called the Pharaohs. Do you remember seeing the Egyptian mummies in the British Museum in London? A mummy is the dead body of a human being or animal to which oils and spices have been applied to prevent it from decaying. The bodies of the Pharaohs were made into mummies when they died and were then placed inside these great pyramids. Near them were placed gold and silver ornaments and furniture and food, because it was thought that they might require them after death. Two or three years ago some people found the body of a Pharaoh, whose name was Tutankhamen, in one of these pyramids. There were many beautiful and valuable things near him.

In Egypt also, in those days, they made fine canals and lakes to take the water for irrigation and agriculture. There was especially the famous Lake Meridu. This shows how clever and advanced the ancient Egyptians were. They must have had fine engineers to build these canals and lakes and the great pyramids.

The little island of Crete or Candia is in the Mediterranean Sea. We passed near it when going from Port Said to Venice. On this little island, there was a fine civilization in the olden days. At Knossos in Crete, there was an enormous palace and we have the remains of this palace still. In this palace there were bathrooms and water pipes, which some ignorant people think are modern inventions. There were also beautiful pottery and sculpture and paintings, and fine metal and ivory work. In this little island of Crete, the people lived peacefully and made great progress.

You must have read of King Midas who got into great difficulties because every thing he touched became gold! He could not eat because his food became gold, and what is the use of gold as food? He was punished for his greed in this way. This is, of course, a fanciful story. It is meant to show us that gold is not such a fine or useful thing as people imagine.

There is another story of Crete which you may have heard. It is about the Minotaur, which is supposed to have been a monster, half man and half bull. It is said that young men and young girls were given to this monster as his food! I have told you before that the idea of religion first came through the fear of the unknown. And because of this fear, not understanding nature and much that happens around us, people used to do many foolish things. It is quite possible that boys and girls were sacrificed in this way not to a real monster, because I do not think such a monster ever existed, but to an imaginary monster!

All over the world, in those ancient days, there was what is called human sacrifice, that is, men and women were sacrificed to imaginary beings whom people worshipped. In Egypt, girls used to be thrown into the river Nile because it was thought that this would please Father Nile.

Fortunately, human sacrifices do not take place now, except perhaps very seldom in some far corner of the world. But even now some people kill animals and sacrifice them to please God! It is a curious way of worshipping anybody.

❒

China and India

We have seen that the early civilizations began and developed in Mesopotamia and Egypt and the little island of Crete in the Mediterranean Sea. About the same time, in China and in India. also, great civilizations began and developed in their own way.

In China, as elsewhere, people settled down in the valleys of great rivers. These people were what are called the Mongolians. They made beautiful vessels out of bronze and later of iron. Canals and fine buildings were made, and a new way of writing was evolved. This writing was quite different from our writing in Hindi or English or Urdu. It was a kind of picture writing. Each word and sometimes even a short sentence was a picture. In ancient Egypt and in Crete and Babylon also, there used to be picture writing. This is now called hieroglyphic writing. You must have seen this writing in the museums and in some books. In Egypt and in the West this writing is only found in very old buildings. Nobody has used this writing there for a very long time. But in China even now, the writing is a kind of picture writing and it is written from top to bottom; not from left to right as in Hindi or English or right to left as in Urdu.

In India, many of the oldest remains of buildings are perhaps still buried in the earth and the sand. They are hidden from us till someone digs them up. But some very old ruins have already been found in the north. We know, however, that long long ago, even before the Aryans came to India, there were Dravidians here, and they had a fine civilization. They used to trade with people in other countries. They sent many of their goods to Mesopotamia and Egypt. Specially they sent across the seas rice and spices, like pepper, and teak wood to build houses. It is said that some of the ancient palaces of the city of Ur in Mesopotamia were made of teak wood which was sent from South India. It is also said that gold and pearls and ivory and peacocks and apes were sent from India to western countries. We thus see that there must have been a great deal of trade between India and other countries in those days. Trade can only exist when people are civilized.

Both in India and China, there were then little states or kingdoms. Neither of these countries was all under one government. Each little city with some villages and fields had a separate government. These are called city states. Many of these were republics even in those early days. There were no kings, only a kind of elected panchayat to govern the state. Some of them, however, were little kingdoms. But although the city states had separate governments, they sometimes cooperated with each other, that is, helped each other. Sometimes one big state became a kind of leader of several smaller states. In China, these small states soon gave place to a great big state, an empire. It was in the days of this empire that the Great Wall of China was built. You have read about this Great Wall and what an enormous thing it is. It was built from the sea to the high mountains in the north to keep off other Mongolian tribes from breaking into China. This wall is 1,400 miles long and is twenty to thirty feet high and twenty-five feet broad. At intervals there are forts and towers in it. If such a wall was built in India it would extend from Lahore in the north to Madras in the south. The Great Wall stands even now, and if you go to China you can see it.

Sea Voyages and Trade

Another interesting people of ancient times were the Phoenicians. They belonged to the same race as the Jews and Arabs. They lived on the western coast of Asia Minor—the Turkey of today. Their chief towns were Acre, Tyre and Sidon on the Mediterranean Sea coast. They were famous for their long journeys by sea for trading purposes. They went all over the Mediterranean Sea and right up to England by sea. They may have come to India also.

We see now two interesting beginnings of great things—sea travel and trade. Each helped the other. There were not, of course, in those days fine steamers and ships like you see today. The first boats must have been simple tree trunks hollowed out. Oars were used with them and sometimes sails to catch the wind. Sea voyages must have been interesting in those days and very exciting. Imagine crossing the Arabian Sea on a little boat with oars and sails! There must have been very little room to move about in it, and the least bit of wind must have made it roll and pitch, and very often it sank. Only brave people would venture out in a boat in the open sea. It was full of risks and for months sometimes they could not see land. If food ran short, they could not get it in the middle of the sea unless they fished or caught a bird. The sea was full of adventure and romance. There are so many stories of sailors and strange happenings in the sea in olden times.

But, in spite of the danger, people went for voyages across the sea. Some may have done it because they loved adventures, but most of them went because of their love of gold and money. For they went for trade—to buy things and sell them. So they made money.

What is trade and how did it begin? Today you see large shops and it is so easy to go inside them and buy what you want. But do you ever think where the things you buy come from? You may buy a woollen shawl in a shop in Allahabad. It may have come all the way from Kashmir and the wool may have grown on the backs of sheep in the mountains of Kashmir or Ladakh. A toothpaste that you buy may have come in ships and railway trains all the way from America. So also you may buy things made in China or Japan or Paris or London. Consider a piece of foreign cloth that is sold in the bazaar here. The cotton grew in India and it was sent to England. A great factory took it and cleaned it and made it into yarn or cotton thread and then into cloth. This cloth then came back again to India and was sold in the bazaar. How many thousands of mile it travelled backwards and forwards before it was offered for sale! It seems rather silly that the cotton that is grown in India had to go all the way to England to be made into cloth and then come back again. This seems such a waste of time and money and energy. It ought to be far cheaper and better to make the cotton into cloth in India. You know that we do not buy or wear foreign cloth. We wear khaddar because it is more sensible to buy things, as far as we can, made in our own country. We also buy and wear khaddar because in this way we help the poor who spin and weave.

So you see that trade is a very complicated thing now. Great ships are always carrying the goods of one country to another. But it was not always so. Right in the early days, when man settled down there was very little trade. Everything that a man wanted he had to get himself or make himself. He did not want much then, of course. Then, as I have already told you, there came a division of labour in the tribe. People did different kinds of work and made different things. Sometimes it must have happened that one tribe had a great deal of one thing and another tribe a great deal of something else. It was natural for them to exchange goods. For instance, one tribe may give a cow for a bag of grain. There was no money in those days. Things could only be exchanged. So exchange began. It must have been rather inconvenient. To get a bag of grain, or something like it, one had to carry a cow or maybe a couple of sheep! But still trade developed.

When gold and silver were found, people started using them for trade. It was easier to carry them. And gradually the custom arose of paying for things in gold and silver. The first person who thought of this must have been a very clever person. This use of gold and silver made trade very much easier. Even then, there were no coins as we have them. Gold used to be weighed in a balance and then given to another person. Much later came coins, and these made trade and exchange still simpler. No weighing was required then as everybody knew the value of a coin. Now money is used everywhere. But we must remember that money is no good by itself. It only helps us to get other things that we want. It helps us to exchange goods. You will remember the story of King Midas who had plenty of gold but nothing to eat! So money is worthless unless it is used to get something that we need.

Even now, however, you will find sometimes in villages that people actually exchange goods, and do not pay money. But generally money is used as it is much more convenient. Some foolish people imagine that money itself is good and they collect and hoard it, instead of using it. This shows that they do not know how money came to be used and what it really is.

❐

Language, Writing and Numerals

We have already considered the various languages and how they are related to each other. Let us think for a while how language must have begun. We find among some animals that there are some words used. The monkeys, it is said, have a few cries or words for simple things. You can also notice the peculiar cries that some animals make when they are frightened and want to warn others of their kind of danger.

Perhaps language started in the same way in man. There must have been very simple cries to begin with—cries of fear and warning. Then, it may be, came what are called labour cries. When a number of people work together they usually make a noise together. Have you not noticed people pulling together at something? Or lifting a great weight together? It seems that all crying together helps them a little. Their labour cries might have been the first words that man used.

Gradually other words must have come in—simple words like water, fire, horse and bear. Probably there were only nouns and no verbs. If a man wanted to say that he had seen a bear he would only say one word 'bear' and point, just like a child. There could hardly be much conversation then!

Language developed. Short sentences came and then longer ones. Probably there was not one language for all the different people at any time. But at some time there could not have been very many different languages. As I have already told you, there were a few languages then, each of which developed a large family of languages.

During the time of the early civilizations, which we have been considering, language had already greatly developed. There were many songs, and bards and singers used to sing them. There was not much writing or books in those days and so people had to remember much more. It is easier to remember rhymes and poetry. Therefore we find that rhymes and ballads were very popular in all these countries where the early civilizations existed.

The singers or bards were especially fond of singing of the glories of dead heroes. People in those days were most interested in fighting and so the songs are about bravery in battle. We find this in India as well as in other countries.

Writing also has had an interesting beginning. I have referred to Chinese writing. All writing must have begun with pictures. A man who wanted to say something about a peacock would try to make a picture or drawing of a peacock. Of course, no one could write much this way. Gradually the pictures would have become simpler and simpler. Much later, an alphabet was thought of and evolved. This immediately made writing far easier and progress became more rapid.

Numerals and counting must have been a great discovery. Without numerals it is difficult to imagine how any kind of business could be done. The person who invented numerals must have been a genius or a very clever person. At first in Europe, numerals were rather clumsy. You know what are called the Roman numerals—I, II, III, IV, V, VI, VII, VIII, IX, X and so on. These are clumsy and difficult to manage. The numerals we use now, in all languages, are very much better. I refer to 1, 2, 3, 4, 5, 6, 7, 8, 9, 10. These are called Arabic numerals because people in Europe got to know them through the Arabs. But the Arabs themselves learnt them from the Indians, so it would be more correct to call them Indian numerals.

But I am going too fast. We have not come to the Arabs yet.

❐

Different Classes of People

Boys and girls, and even grown-ups, are often taught history in a peculiar way. They learn the names of kings and others, and dates of battle and the like. But surely history does not consist of battle and a few persons who became kings and generals. History should tell us of the people of a country; how they lived, what they did, and what they thought. It should tell us of their joys and sorrows; of their difficulties and how they overcame them. And if we study history in this way we can learn a lot from it. If we have to face the same kind of difficulty or trouble, our reading of history may help us to get over it. Especially, our study of past times will help us in finding out if people have been getting better and better or worse; if there has been progress or not.

Of course, one must try to learn something from the lives of great men and women of past times. But we must also try to learn what the condition of various kinds of people in olden days was.

I have written to you many letters. This is the twenty-fourth of the series. But so far we have only discussed very old times about which we do not know much. We can hardly call this history. We may if we like call it the beginning of history, or the dawn of history. Soon we shall consider the later periods about which we know more and which may be called the historical times. But before we leave the early civilizations, let us have another peep into them and see what different kinds of people lived in those days.

We have already seen how in the early tribes people started doing different kinds of work. There was division of work or labour. We have also seen how the leader of the tribe, the patriarch, separated his family from the others, and only did the managing part of the work. He became a higher kind of person, or we may say that his family belonged to a different class from the other people. Thus we find two classes of people—one doing the managing and ordering, and the other doing the actual work. And of course the class doing the managing part had much more power and they used this to take as many things as possible. They became richer as they took more and more from the others who worked.

And so, as division of work went on, several classes arose. There was the king and his family and people of his court. They did the work of managing the country and fighting for it. They usually did no other work.

Then there were the priests in temples and all other people attached to the temples. They were very important persons in those days and we will consider their work again.

Thirdly, there were the merchants. These were the traders who carried the goods of one country to another, who bought and sold, and opened shops.

Fourthly, there were the artisans, that is the people who made all kinds of things, who spun yarn and wove cloth, who made pottery and brass goods and articles of gold and ivory, and many other things. Most of these people lived in or near towns, but there were many in the villages also.

Lastly, there were the peasants and labourers who worked in the fields and in the cities. This was, of course, the largest class. All the other classes tried to get something out of them.

❐

Kings and Temples and Priests

We saw in our last letter that five different classes were formed. The biggest class was that of the peasants and labourers. The peasants ploughed the land and tilled the soil and grew the food. If the peasantry had not done so and no one else had worked on the land, there would have been no food, or at any rate very little food. So the peasants were very important. Without them, everybody would have starved. The labourers also did useful work on the land and in the towns. But although these people did such important work, and were so necessary to everybody, they got very little out of it. Most of what they produced went to others, especially to the king and his class of people, including the nobles.

The king and his class, as we have seen, had a great deal of power. During the days of the early tribes the land belonged to the whole tribe, and not to any one person. But as the king's class grew in power, they said that the land belonged to them. They became the landlords, and the peasants, who really did all the hard work on the land, became merely their servants in a way. Whatever the peasants produced from the land was divided—a big share going to the landlord.

Some of the temples also had land and were thus landlords.

Let us see what these temples and their priests were. In one of my letters to you I said that the early savage men started thinking of god and religion because they did not understand many things and were afraid of what they did not understand. They made a god or goddess of everything—a river, a mountain, the sun, trees, animals and things which they could not see but only imagined, like spirits. Because they were afraid, they always thought that their gods wanted to punish them. Their gods were, like themselves, harsh and cruel, and the people were always trying to appease them or please them by sacrifices.

Temples grew up for these gods. Inside the temple, there was a special room called a shrine or holy place, where there was an image of the god they worshipped. They could not worship something they could not see. This is a little difficult. You know that a little child can usually think of things it sees. The early people were like children somewhat. And as they could not worship without images, they put images in their temples. It is curious that these images were usually horribly ugly—animals or sometimes half animal and half man. In Egypt, they worshipped at one time a cat and at another period, I think, a monkey. Why people should worship these awful images of animals it is very difficult to understand. If an image is to be worshipped, why not make it beautiful? But perhaps the idea was that the gods were something to be afraid of and so they were made into these terrible images. At that time, probably, people did not think of one god or one great power, as most people think now. They imagined that there were a large number of gods and goddesses, sometimes even quarrelling with each other. Different cities and different countries often had different gods to worship.

The temples were full of priests and priestesses. Usually the priests knew reading and writing and were more learned than the others. They became therefore the advisers of the kings. The books in those days were written or copied by the priests. Because they had some knowledge, they were the wise men of old. They were the doctors also. And often just to show people how clever they were, they showed them some tricks to impose upon them. The people were very simple and ignorant, and considered the priests magicians and were frightened of them.

The priests mixed with the life of the people in every way. They were the wise men and everyone went to them when he was in trouble or was ill. They arranged big festivals for the people. There were no calendars in those days, specially for the common people. They counted by festivals.

The priests often deluded and misled the people. But they helped them also in many ways and made them progress.

It is possible that in some places when the people first settled down in towns, the people who governed them were priests and not kings. Later the king came and displaced the priest as he could fight better. In some places, the same person was king and priest, like the Pharaohs in Egypt. Pharaohs indeed were considered half divine or half god even when alive. When they died, they were worshipped as gods.

❐

A Look Back

Are you not quite tired of my letters! I think you deserve a rest. Well, I shall not write to you anything new for some time. I want you just to think over what we have already done. We have rushed through millions of years in a few letters. Starting from the time when the earth was a bit of the sun, we saw how it separated and slowly cooled down. The moon then shot off. For long ages, there was no life. Then during millions and millions of years—have you any idea how long a time a million years is?—life grew very slowly. It is enormously difficult to be able to form an idea of millions of years. You are only ten years old and how grown-up and old you are! You are a *jeune fille, n'est-ce pas*? A young lady! A hundred years to you is a terribly long time. And then a thousand! And a million, which is a thousand times thousand! I am afraid we cannot get this in our little heads properly. We imagine that we are so important and little things annoy us and worry us. But what are these little happenings in the long history of the world? It does us good to read and learn something of these vast periods of history because we will not then worry about little things much.

Let us remember the tremendously long time during which there was no life at all; and then of the long time when there were only animals in the sea. There is no man anywhere on earth. The animals come and roam about for millions of years with no man to shoot and kill them. And when at last man comes, he is a puny, tiny, little thing, the weakest of animals. Slowly in thousands of years, he becomes stronger and cleverer till he becomes the master animal on earth. All the other animals become his servants and slaves to do as he tells them.

Then we come to the growth of civilization. We have seen the early beginnings of it. We shall try to follow it in later times. We have not got millions of years to go through now. In our letters, we have arrived at a period which was only about four or five thousand years ago. But we know more about these four thousand years than about the millions of years that went before. The history and growth of man really took place during these four thousand years. You will read about this history a great deal when you grow up. I shall only write a little about it, just to give you some idea of what has happened to man in this little world of ours.

❐

Fossils and Ruins

I have not written to you for a long time. In my last two letters, we were looking back on the ancient periods which we have been considering in our letters. I sent you some picture postcards of fossil fishes to give you some idea of what these fossils were like. In Mussoorie, when we met, I showed you pictures of other fossils.

You may remember especially the fossil reptiles. Reptiles are usually animals which crawl, like the snakes, lizards, crocodiles and turtles, which we have today. The reptiles in old days belonged to the same family but were very different and were very big. You will remember the enormous brutes we saw in the South Kensington Museum. One of them was thirty to forty feet long. There was also a kind of frog bigger than a man, and a tortoise almost as big. Enormous bats used to fly about, and one animal, the iguanodon, when it stood up on its feet was as big as a small tree.

You also saw fossils of old plants. There were beautiful fern markings in the rock, and leaves and palms.

Long after the reptiles came the mammals or the animals which suckle or give milk to their young. Most of the animals we see around us, and we ourselves, are also mammals. The mammals of old times were not very different from some of our animals today. They were often bigger, but not so big as the reptiles used to be. There were elephants with enormous tusks and huge bears.

You also saw remains of fossil man. These were not very interesting as they were usually bones and skulls. More interesting were the flint instruments which early men used to make.

I also showed you some fine pictures of Egyptian tombs and mummies. Some of these, you will remember, were very beautiful. On the wooden coffins were painted long stories of people. Very interesting were the wall paintings from the Egyptian tombs at Thebes.

You also saw pictures of the ruins of palaces and temples at Thebes in Egypt. Huge buildings they were, with enormous pillars. Near Thebes is the colossus of Memnon, an enormous statue.

There were also pictures of the ruined temples and buildings at Karnak in Upper Egypt. Even from these ruins, you can form some idea of how mighty the old Egyptians were as builders. They could not have built these great temples and palaces unless they knew a great deal of engineering.

We have now finished our brief look back. In our next letter we shall go ahead.

❐

The Aryans Come to India

So far we have discussed very, very old times. We shall now see how man developed and what he did. All these old times are called pre-historic, that is before history, as we have no real history of that period. We have to guess a lot. We are now on the verge or edge of history.

Let us see what happened in India first. We have already seen that in the very old times India, like Egypt, had a civilization. There was trade, and ships carried Indian goods to Egypt and Mesopotamia and other countries. In those days the people who lived in India were called Dravidians. They are the people whose descendants live in South India now, around Madras.

The Dravidians were invaded by the Aryans from the north. There must have been enormous numbers of these Aryan peoples in Central Asia and not finding enough food there for all, they spread out to other countries. They went in large numbers to Persia and even to Greece further west. They also came to India in crowds over the mountains near Kashmir.

The Aryans were a strong fighting people and they drove the Dravidians before them. Wave after wave of the Aryans must have come to India from the north-west. Perhaps, at first, the Dravidians stopped them, but when more and more came they could not be stopped. For long, the Aryans remained in the north, only in Afghanistan and the Punjab. Then they came further down to what are now called the United Provinces, where we live. They went on spreading till they came to the Vindhya mountains in central India. It was difficult to cross these as there were thick forests. So for a long time the Aryans remained on the northern side of the Vindhya mountains. Many of them managed to cross them and went to the south, but crowds could not go, and so the south remained chiefly Dravidian.

It is very interesting to study the coming of the Aryans to India. You can find out a lot about them from our old Sanskrit books. Some of these, like the Vedas, must have been written about that time. The oldest Veda is the Rig Veda and you can form some idea from it of the part of India which the Aryans occupied then. From the other Vedas and other old Sanskrit books like the Puranas we find how the Aryans went on spreading. Perhaps you do not know much about these ancient books. When you grow up you will know more. But even now you know many stories which have come out of the Puranas. Much later came the great book the Ramayana, and later the Mahabharata.

From these books we find that when the Aryans lived only in the Punjab and in Afghanistan they called this part 'Brahmavarta'. Afghanistan was then called 'Gandhara'. Do you remember Gandhari in the Mahabharata? She was called so because she came from Gandhara or Afghanistan.

Afghanistan now is a separate country from India, but in those days both were one country.

When the Aryans came further down to the plains of the Ganga and Jumna they named all northern India 'Aryavarta'.

Like the other people of olden times, they settled down in cities on the banks of rivers. Kashi or Benares, Prayag and so many other cities are situated on river banks.

❒

What were the Aryans in India Like?

The Aryans must have come to India five or six thousand years ago, or perhaps even more. Of course they did not all come in a bunch. Army after army, tribe after tribe, family after family, must have come for hundreds of years. Imagine them travelling in long caravans with all their household goods laden on carts or on the backs of animals. They did not come as tourists do nowadays. There was no going back for them. They came to stay, or fight and die. Most of them, as I have told you, came over the mountains of the north-west. But perhaps some came by sea also from the Persian Gulf and went in their little ships up the river Indus.

What were these Aryans like? We can find out a lot about them from the books they wrote. Some of these books, like the Vedas, are perhaps the oldest books in the world. Probably they were not written down to begin with. They were learnt by heart and recited and chanted to others. They are written in such beautiful Sanskrit that you can almost sing them. Even now it is a pleasure to hear a man with a good voice, who knows Sanskrit, recite the Vedas.

The Vedas are considered very holy books by Hindus. But what does the word Vedas mean? It means knowledge. And the Vedas contained the knowledge which the wise men of those days, called rishis and munis, had gathered. They did not have railways and telegraphs and cinemas in those days. But that does not mean that they were ignorant. Some people think that the wise men of old were wiser than any today. But whether they were wiser or not, they wrote wonderful books which even today are greatly admired. This itself shows how great these men of the olden days must have been.

As I have said, these Vedas were not at first written. They were remembered and were handed down from generation to generation by word of mouth. They must have had wonderful memories in those days. How many of us can learn by heart whole books?

Those days when the Vedas were written are called the Vedic perod. The first Veda is the *Rig Veda*. It is full of hymns and songs which the old Aryans used to sing. They must have been a very light-hearted people, not morose and gloomy but full of joy and adventure. And in their joy they made beautiful songs and sang them out to the gods they worshipped.

They were very proud of themselves and their race. The very word 'Arya' meant a gentleman, a superior kind of person. And they loved freedom greatly. They were not like their descendants in India today who have little courage and hardly feel the loss of their freedom. To the Aryans of old, death was better than dishonour or slavery.

They were good fighters, and they knew something of science and a great deal of agriculture. They naturally attached great value to agriculture and so they valued also everything that helped agriculture. The great rivers gave them water, and they loved them and looked upon them as great friends and benefactors. The bull and cow helped them also very much both in agriculture and in their daily lives, for the cow gave milk which was valued very greatly. So they specially cared for these animals and sang their praises. Long afterwards, people, forgetting the real reason for the care of the cow, started worshipping her as if that was any good to anybody.

The Aryans, being very proud of themselves, were afraid of getting mixed up with the other inhabitants of India. So they made laws and rules to prevent this mixture, so that Aryans could not marry the others. Long afterwards, this developed into the caste system, as it is called today. Now of course, it has become perfectly ridiculous. Some people are afraid of touching others or eating with others. Fortunately, this is getting less and less now.

❒

The Ramayana and the Mahabharata

After the Vedic Age in India, when the Vedas were written, came what is called the Epic Age. It is called the Epic Age because two great epics, that is long poems telling us the stories of great heroes, were written then. These two books were the Ramayana and the Mahabharata, which you know.

During the Epic Age, the Aryans had spread out all over Northern India up to the Vindhya mountains. All this land was called 'Aryavarta', as I have told you. What is the United Provinces now was called the Madhyadesha, the middle country. Bengal was called Vanga.

Now there is an interesting fact which you may like to know. If you look at the map of India and imagine where Aryavarta must have been, between the Himalayas and the Vindhya mountains, you will see it is rather like a crescent moon. Therefore Aryavarta was also called the land of the Moon. Indu means moon and so Aryavarta was Induland.[1]

The Aryans were very fond of the crescent moon. They considered all crescent-shaped places especially holy. Many

[1] Indira's pet name was Indu.

of their great cities were crescent-shaped, like Benares. Even in Allahabad, I wonder if you know that the Ganga makes a crescent.

The Ramayana, as you know, is the story of Ramchandra and Sita and of their fight against Ravana, king of Lanka, that is now Ceylon. The original story is written in Sanskrit by Valmiki. Many other versions were written later in other languages. The best known is Tulsidas's in Hindi, called the '*Rama Charita Manas*'.

In the Ramayana, we are told that Rama was helped by monkeys in South India and Hanuman was the great hero of the monkeys. It may be that the story of the Ramayana is really a story of the fights of the Aryans against the people of the south whose leader was Ravana.

The Ramayana is full of beautiful stories but I cannot refer to them here. You must read them for yourself.

The Mahabharata came long after the Ramayana. It is a much bigger book. It tells not of the fight between Aryans and Dravidians but of a great fight between Aryans and Aryans. But apart from the fight, it is a wonderful book, full of great ideas and noble stories. Above all, it is dear to all of us because of that jewel of a poem which it contains—the Bhagavad Gita.

These were the books written in India thousands of years ago. Who but the greatest of men could have written them? And although they were written so long ago, they live today in India and every child knows of them and every grown-up is influenced by them.

❑❑❑

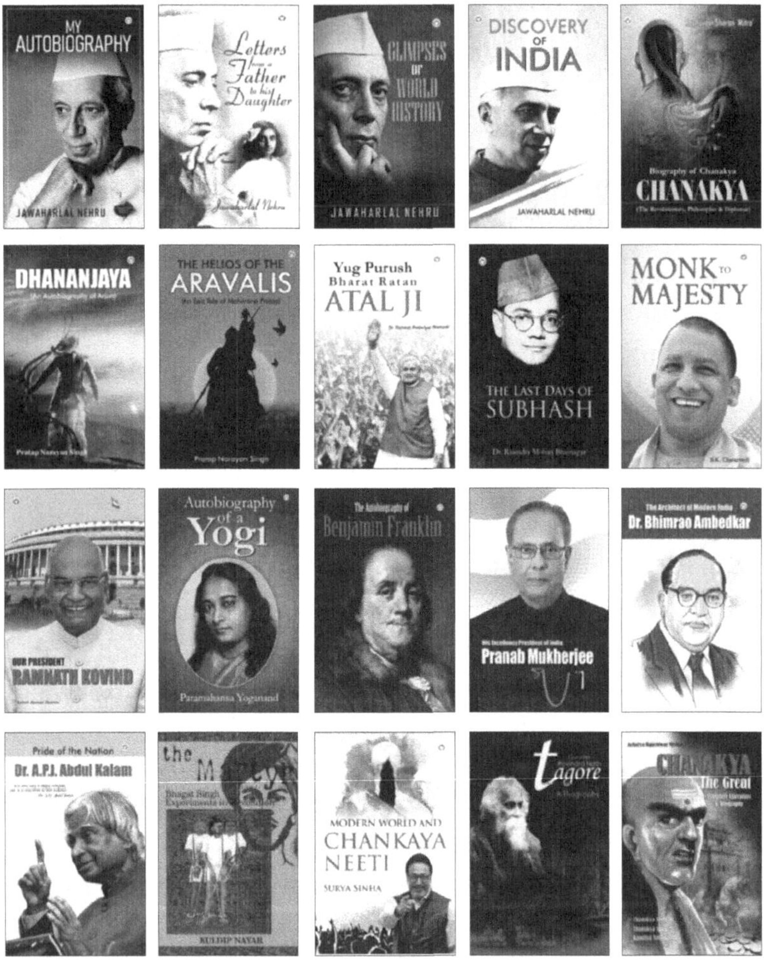

MY AUTOBIOGRAPHY
JAWAHARLAL NEHRU
Letters from a Father to his Daughter
GLIMPSES OF WORLD HISTORY
JAWAHARLAL NEHRU
DISCOVERY OF INDIA
JAWAHARLAL NEHRU
Biography of Chanakya
CHANAKYA
DHANANJAYA
THE HELIOS OF THE ARAVALIS
Yug Purush Bharat Ratan ATAL JI
THE LAST DAYS OF SUBHASH
MONK TO MAJESTY
OUR PRESIDENT RAMNATH KOVIND
Autobiography of a Yogi
Paramahansa Yogananda
The Autobiography of Benjamin Franklin
Pranab Mukherjee
The Architect of Modern India
Dr. Bhimrao Ambedkar
Pride of the Nation
Dr. A.P.J. Abdul Kalam
KULDIP NAYAR
MODERN WORLD AND CHANKAYA NEETI
SURYA SINHA
tagore
CHANAKYA The Great